PRIMERS

Volume Four

Dear Martin,
Hope this book finds you
well. Thanks!

Lewis ...

PRIMERS

Volume Four

Lewis Buxton
Amelia Loulli
Victoria Richards

Nine
Arches
Press

Primers: Volume Four
Lewis Buxton, Amelia Loulli and Victoria Richards
Selecting Editors: Kim Moore and Jane Commane

ISBN: 978-1-911027-71-3
eISBN: 978-1-911027-77-5

First published April 2019 by:

Nine Arches Press
Unit 14, Sir Frank Whittle Business Centre,
Great Central Way, Rugby.
CV21 3XH
United Kingdom

www.ninearchespress.com

Printed in the United Kingdom by:
Imprint Digital

Nine Arches Press is supported using public funding by Arts Council England.

Supported using public funding by
ARTS COUNCIL ENGLAND

PRIMERS

Volume Four

is produced in partnership with:

About the Selecting Editors:

Kim Moore's first full-length collection *The Art of Falling* was published by Seren in 2015 and was awarded the 2016 Geoffrey Faber Memorial Prize. Her poem 'In That Year' from the collection was shortlisted for the Forward Prize for Best Published Poem. She won a Northern Writers Award in 2014, an Eric Gregory Award in 2011 and the Geoffrey Dearmer Prize in 2010. Her pamphlet *If We Could Speak Like Wolves* was a winner in the 2012 Poetry Business Pamphlet Competition, and went on to be shortlisted for a Michael Marks Award and named in *The Independent* as a Book of the Year. She was chosen to take part in Versopolis, a European funded scheme to promote young poets at festivals across Europe and following this her work has been translated into several languages. She is one of the judges for the 2018 National Poetry Competition and is currently a PhD candidate at Manchester Metropolitan University, working on her second collection.

Jane Commane is a poet, editor and publisher. Her first full-length collection, *Assembly Lines,* was published by Bloodaxe in 2018. In 2016, she was chosen to join Writing West Midlands' Room 204 writer development programme. A graduate of the Warwick Writing Programme, for a decade she also worked in museums and archives. Jane is editor at Nine Arches Press, co-editor of *Under the Radar* magazine, and is co-author, with Jo Bell, of *How to Be a Poet,* a creative writing handbook (Nine Arches Press). In 2017, she was awarded a Jerwood Compton Poetry Fellowship.

Contents

Victoria Richards

FOREWORD

Primers is a collaboration between the Poetry School and Nine Arches Press. It is a unique mentoring and publication scheme, which aims to identify, teach, edit, publish, and publicise the very best emerging poets.

It combines the Poetry School's long experience in the teaching of poetry with Nine Arches' expertise in editing and publishing beautiful and original books. In each iteration, the Poetry School, Jane Commane of Nine Arches Press, and a guest mentor – this year, the Geoffrey Faber Award-winning poet Kim Moore – select three poets we believe to be on the cusp of something special.

These three poets receive intensive mentoring to find and shape their voices, work closely on editing a pamphlet-length selection of poems and appear together in the book you're holding in your hand – *Primers: Volume Four.*

Previous winners have included Geraldine Clarkson, Cynthia Miller and Romalyn Ante, and Primers poets have gone on to win the *Poetry London* Prize (twice!), the Manchester Creative Writing Prize, and the Saboteur Award, to be PBS Pamphlet Choices, be featured in *Vogue,* and run national poetry festivals and innovative publishing houses. They are, in short, ones to watch. And this year's crop is no exception.

Lewis Buxton's poems are fearless in their exploration of masculinity and the toxic ways it is performed in and by society. These are unusual poems in that the gaze of the poet is fixed on the male body and its vulnerability, from the 'tennis racket' body of a brother, the quarterback with 'five concussions in fourteen months' or the porn star looking down at the 'moon' of his stomach. These poems often break free of the constraint of punctuation, using the line break and the white space of the poem to de-familiarise the way we see not just the male body, but the way men move through the world.

Amelia Loulli's poems are also rooted in the territory of the body, carrying at their heart a belief in the power of language to make sense and connections between grief, violence and trauma. Motherhood is figured as both presence and absence when she writes 'Absence / especially the maternal kind / is only a mirror for the left-behind / to look for themselves in.' These poems take a searing, unflinching look at complex feelings around motherhood, whilst interrogating the relationship between mothers and daughters, and what it means to be both.

On the surface, Victoria Richards' poetry may seem to cover similar concerns in its exploration of how the self is both lost and found in motherhood but her approach to language is very different. She takes the reader on a rollercoaster ride with her use of long, tumbling sentences and similes pushed to their extremes. Desire in all its outrageousness figures prominently. When she writes that she wants to roll Ingrid Bergman's 'eyes / against my tongue / like that gobstopper I kept for weeks in a plastic pot of precious things' in one poem, and then in another, writes about wanting to 'sit in the quiet dark, in a ghost dress of my own', we are left with no choice but to believe her.

It is both this variety and convergence that is at the heart of Primers – and exactly what makes the selection process so unique and exciting. Each of these three poets explores themes of the body, gender, grief, and how we find our way through transformative, ever-moving experiences in a world that tries to 'fix' us to a limited point of reference with its expectations; yet each poet also found a different way in to see these ideas and matters afresh. So much is about the combination of voices: what they have to say in their own right and what they tell us together, in chorus.

The selection process for this fourth volume presented us with plenty to consider; which poems did we love, and which ones intrigued us, surprised us, or called us back to spend more time with them – and vitally, which had the potential to flourish further with the addition of mentoring and editing time? Our conversations around the longlist, then the shortlist, were animated and thoroughly enjoyable, because we felt we had such a rich selection to choose from.

We must also highlight the seven other shortlisted poets, who all presented us with adventurous and ambitious new work: Charlotte Baldwin, Valerie Bence, Rachel Burns, Sally Davis, Olga Dermott-Bond, Nina Mingya Powles and Anna Selby. There was clearly a very talented field of poets this year to select from, and we fully expect to see more than a few of these poets going on to make their mark in years to come. It should be a note of encouragement also, to anyone thinking of entering Primers in future, or who has done so in the past and not been selected, to know that Amelia Loulli was shortlisted for *Primers: Volume Three* and is now, joyfully, presented here as one of our final three poets in *Primers: Volume Four*. A huge well done to everyone who took the plunge in 2018 and entered this most recent scheme – and a wish to you all to keep writing and keep taking your work forward.

And finally, our hearty congratulations to Lewis Buxton, Amelia Loulli and Victoria Richards. We are thrilled to be presenting your striking, electrifying poems together, and wish them many appreciative readers.

April 2018
Ali Lewis, Poetry School
Kim Moore, Selecting Editor
Jane Commane, Nine Arches Press

Lewis Buxton

Born in London in 1993, **Lewis Buxton** is a poet, performer and arts producer. His poems have appeared in *Ambit, Ink, Sweat & Tears* and *Oxford Poetry* as well as coming third in the *Magma* Poetry Prize. He lives in Norwich.

&

& looks like a body,
the head, then the round stomach, like me
stood in the shower, my belly
pushing against itself, my head
held in place
by the loops
&
lines of my neck.
I am tied together, except for the tail
of the ampersand: coccyx, or undone belt,
gesturing outwards, the body buckling –
man & *boy, love* & *hurt* – the last tail opening like a wound.
I look down at my ampersand body, all the things I am & & & &
a row of me in the barbers' mirrors thrown back & forth
like a rugby ball – ampersand is fingers crossed for luck,
ampersand is a noose, unwound, untied,
ampersand is trying to hold everything together & & & &
in doing so is
falling
apart

punctuation knots itself around my neck
until
I cannot breathe anymore

Tense

Hugging my brother
is like holding a tennis racket
to your chest

his ribs
taut strings
his shoulder blades arch

like a racket's frame
the tendons in his neck
stretch against the skin.

Thin as he is I find it
difficult to fit
language around him.

I worry about
the world pressing
down on his body.

When I hug him
I am careful
of his ribs

the breath beneath.
I remind myself
this is not a game.

Mackerel Fishing

The sky's hair is flecked with grey
and fishermen are showing us

how to hook a life
spear it through the mouth

lift it breathless onto the deck.
My brother is first to catch a mackerel.

Cold & twitching, we celebrate
the last minutes of its life

whilst Dad sits apart, his hands
gripping the bench, knuckles white,

shaking like an engine,
taking long, deep breaths.

He'd wanted to catch a fish,
to run his hands through water,

scoop the grey-blue in his palm
but now he won't talk to anyone.

We pretend we haven't noticed
and turn our eyes back to the sea.

Advice from the Quarterback

It can be easy to hide. Five concussions
in fourteen months. *Just keep your mouth shut*
and your head down, test the limit of your bone.
Stay away from people who'd think you have one, keep quiet,

just try to go out there and function as all men do,
day after day, our ears ringing from colliding
so hard with the world. Sometimes I get
so angry, so blind. *Everybody knows it*

is a dangerous game, padded rage hurtling at you
the fear before connection. But *the game has done
so much for me,* filled my blood with grit & cortisone,
it's made me who I am. My father said he worries

that I am *so tough, such a competitor,* that I might say
I'm O.K when I'm not O.K. I mustn't worry
after throwing five hundred yards & four touchdowns
in a 40-37 victory, *that I barely remember the game.*

A&E

The doctor's been busy with heart attacks.
She's been washing the blood stuff
of Sunday night from her hands. This morning
a man is a sink plugged full of shame
and she has to find the best way
to hold his body, to bind his limbs
and adjust to the angle where he is most yawning
so she can pull out what is stuck
at the very base of him. Comfort
is no longer an option. He is lifted like a baby
having its nappy changed,
whilst his girlfriend waits
in the hall, wondering if he was elastic
enough when she slipped *it* in.
Was it the danger it posed that excited him?
Or did he feel like he was giving birth? Certainly
this was what made him feel alive. I love most
that it was a Monday when he found the pulse
of the morning, before work
when he wanted to bring some joy to his body.
He couldn't wait till the weekend to feel
the world move slightly inside him.

Nom-de-guerre

'Someone starts a game which gives us
a porn-star's nom-de-guerre. It calls
for mothers' maiden names, involves first pets…'
– Tiffany Atkinson

Not even my mother would recognise me
from this angle: how I see myself, straight down
looking over the moon of my stomach.

I'm no Jon Dough, Peter North or Tommy Gunn
but I still see through a screen, me in another life,
the knot & stitch of my body pulled tight to the camera

making sure I'm well developed. In this life
I go like clockwork, hard rock & tick tock
stopped only by the yell of *cut* –

how much of my body is left
in the editing suite? The camera follows me
from the set, catches me on my off days

when I'm not ready to fuck: sweating
unscripted & flaccid. How will I be christened
with only a cock and three blunt syllables to my name?

Red Shirt

after Robert Pinsky

The collar, the colour: red checks,
the seams coming undone,
your skin through open buttons,

the missing ones don't matter now
because this is just the shirt
you sleep in and I dream about.

The length fits you
like a dress, the thickness, warm
as another body on week nights.

The sleeves, the rolled cuffs.
I fall asleep in your bed, my arm turning
to a ghost beneath your body.

The hems, the loose stitches
fluttering like split ends, how you
move into my touch.

The moment when you take it off,
bare as a light bulb, your skin
a cold moon, and you are looking at me

like something wonderful or terrible
is happening and in this light
you won't tell me which.

Frightened Rabbit

Gone boy, boy lost but still running, trainers pounding the ground, looking for a river: frightened rabbit, Richey Edwards & Jeff Buckley. *No, this can't be the way it ends.*

Chandler from Friends, Ross not knowing how to be lonely because we can't all fuck like Joey. We so rarely know our bodies; we might drown in our own blood stream.

Wiped clean surfaces. Blood, sunlight, darkness sits with you in the pub. Grab life by the free porn. Wine & whisky & clean white shirts that don't show the hurt.

Our bodies are piano keys that girls press softly. They are rubbing the skin from our knuckles whilst we beg for attention. One study reveals a rise in men with erectile dysfunction.

Fist-language, knuckles leave speech marks: torn shirts, Die Hard, wife-beater vests. We know our best-dressed heroes by what they have done to their partners. Frightened rabbits, fights in the street.

Why me? Cry, football, cry, rugby. *This is the first time you've hugged me.* Granddad in the navy, boy in the club, we all have tequila salt in our wounds, baby.

Punch drunk, hunched up, dumb luck, club shuts. The battery on our phones runs red as blood, shout when you think you've had enough, we will keep going anyway.

We need to talk gut, but what we talk is bullshit, dog bark, frightened rabbit. Language is beyond our grasp and we would be talking too loud in all this music. Men all put their hands to the earth and say sorry *but*.

We know that our muscles look best in shadow, sweet as bruised apples. Stressed millennial, moisturiser & shaving cream, cut throat razors trying to save us from ourselves.

Pink button down, garish tie. *Every colour does some violence to the eye*; every father does some violence to the boy; every boy does some violence to themselves. *Dying is safer than saying what I feel.*

Shrug on coats of muscle, bulletproof denim, bad dreams & broken ankles, depression battles fought with toy swords & water pistols. *Get your prostate checked.*

Pray, look up to heaven, brave new haircut: David Beckham. Barber shaved too close to the skin, you can see our raw pinkness, our baby faces. We cut ourselves on blades of grass, the world a knife held to our throats.

Sleep Apnoea

for Eddie Hall

The world's strongest man
often stops breathing in his sleep.
He's so big he needs a machine
to carry his breath for him.

He can pull trains with his teeth,
deadlift trees, bicep curl cars –
still he dreams of raising
aeroplanes above his head,
of bench-pressing the sky.

His eyeballs have popped
out of their sockets from the strain,
like soap from wet hands.
His deltoids have been sucked
from pockets of bone.

Smaller men carry their children
like balloons, keep their wives awake
with the depth of their snores
but he tears phonebooks in half
because he has no one left to call.

His heart is a dumbbell
being lifted to a heavy beat,
and at night he cannot feel himself
holding his breath too long.

Bruises

football   **fell climbing a lamppost**   **Liam's elbow**

one at the hinge of me
feels like   breathlessness   colour of dusk

when mum sees she says,   *You've been in the wars*

splinter   **red brick wall**   **science desk**

I feel proud   what she means is

get used to bandages   *your body is not as buoyant as expected*

door step   **pinched skin**   **hammer & wood work**

in the bath I count them all   thirteen this week   I think they're pretty

a boy called Patrick   **fly kick**   **changing rooms**

my shins are a watercolour   lilies or   bluebells in Spring

Taxidermy

The girl at the party holds aloft her stuffed capuchin
and explains how you cut straight down the middle, suck
out the organs, like a foot coming out of a sock of skin,

then you stitch it back together. The brain, you dry up
with a chemical so it won't rot. Former Mr California
Rich Piana, collapsed at 45 whilst having a haircut.

At the autopsy they found his heart and liver
were twice the weight of a regular man's. They sliced
into him, opened his sternum to see his lungs and I wonder

if they thought of stuffing him? Freezing his blue-white
eyes and bleached grin, putting his body on show
looking more real than he ever did in life.

Shadow Boxing

the boy fighting ghosts // in his back garden will never know // that his punches // have landed in my poem // in the skin & bone of winter // dressed in a string vest and cotton bottom shorts // he works the body of nothingness // his gloves glancing off the cheekbone of air // breaking December's icy jaw // he rests hands on thighs // trying to catch the breath // that keeps disappearing from his lungs // does he think // about what he is punching // is the swing enough // the air resistance // I write every jab and twitch // reach out towards him // trying to catch something before it hits // the ground // a boy who doesn't know // what he is hitting // let alone why

Sevenling

I dress like my idea of a boy:
creased trousers & pea coats & good shoes,
things the world expects of me.

I'd love to paint my eyes & nails
& skin, the colour of dusk & blood & sky
be beautiful for a moment, dropping

expectations like a coat on a dance floor.

Cues

for Tom

The pub's red and yellow glow holds us still,
our beer sitting cheap and quiet at our elbows.
Even the green stubble of the pool table outgrows
our beards and in this light, we're beautiful.
Our bodies look for angles, negotiating shots,
I break the triangle's neat silence and we hear
the click of colours against one another.
We learn when to be powerful, when to be soft.
I want to win but not for this to end, not now,
when I'm passing the last cue left on the shelf
to a boy I'm so close with I could be playing myself.
The knock of white on red, the hum of yellow
rolling to the edge, the scrape of cue and blue chalk.
I want to notice the space that's left and fill it with our talk.

Amelia Loulli

Amelia Loulli is a writer and actor living in Cumbria. Her poetry has been twice shortlisted for the Bridport Prize, awarded second place in the Battered Moons Poetry Competition and longlisted for the *London Magazine* Poetry Prize. A member of the Kendal Brewery Poets, she was also shortlisted for *Primers: Volume Three.*

Rock-a-bye Baby

Once, my sister died, and Mum and Dad
were swapped
with players who pretended that food
could still be swallowed, and nights were still
for sleeping
and only the way they said my name, as though
its syllables were wrong, as though it ended
the wrong way
could prove what I knew: none of them
were coming back.

       What happened to her body is
they burned it
on a bonfire, like when the Guy gets scorched
every black November. I had to stay behind, still
very much alive
and arrange myself small among the sofa cushions
trying to hide, hoping I might trick them and they would
come home,
tired and smelling of charcoal.

       Afterwards, nothing was said
of her toes,
how small they must have been inside a box that big. I imagined
they would have counted them, a habit is a habit after all,
this little piggy
so still, and never tickled, and they never once forgot
to buy cereal, or to collect me from school, but sometimes
when they thought
I was sleeping, they stood together behind my bedroom door,
silent and hidden and crying in time to every nursery rhyme
      I'd ever been sung…

       Baby, baby, where have you gone?
baby, baby, please come home, baby, baby,
we kept the wrong one.

When I Was Little

Mum smoked the cigarettes
and Dad kept the guns
and this was the best way around

because Mum had *destruction*
tattooed on her breast bone and Dad
kept himself to himself.

And I weighed myself at 6pm
every Tuesday to see
what I continued to be made of

which was only ever a bit
of both of them
and too much of everything else.

And the loft housed a creature called Boris
who heard my secrets at night
and made me run fast as a bullet

up the stairs beneath his hatch
and sometimes when I sat on the loo
and bent my head to the left

I could see his fingers trying to escape.
So I closed the door but the light was broken
and the girls at school all told me

we couldn't be friends unless I was brave.
Brave enough to stand in front
of the blackened mirror and chant

Bloody Mary, Bloody Mary, thirteen times
to the wicked Queen's face.
And once when I screamed,

Dad slapped me so hard across my cheek,
his fingers stayed there, red as menses for days,
and mum laughed like a film star

through clouds of her own smoke,
every time I told her
I was afraid.

Something in the Blood

like the inhibitor you don't have
the inhibitor
which makes you swell
but never bruise

which has never stopped you
throwing yourself
at hard things
walls and doors

and even harder things
which show themselves
in your fists
like balloons

filled with sand
your inflated face
none of us recognise

so much more
lips and skin
than we have ever seen

and the words you spit
when Dad removes
the spoon handle

which he slides
lubricated with tears
straight down your throat

to lever open airways
to buy
more time

just so you can tell him
once your voice
has enough passage
to escape

his hands
smell of piss
and dirty money

Love Your Daughters

"Live or die, but don't poison everything."
– Anne Sexton

Not your garden with its bullish birds,
not your daughters

or your sons,
especially not your daughters,

don't poison those.
Eyes like glass pearls

behind their bed covers,
your girls with babies

hidden beneath them
like toys with plastic hair,

the babies they learn to hold
to their raw breasts,

the daughters with blood and milk
sealed up in lunch bags, waiting

for midday, the daughters
with horses and castles

embroidered with golden threads
into simple cotton, the ones you paid for

though nobody thanked you, thank you
Mother. Now please, the Doctor

didn't insist you feed them yourself, alone
and leaking, he didn't even say

you had to stay. Absence,
especially the maternal kind,

is only a mirror for the left-behind
to look for themselves in.

I know your yellowing hands,
impatient fingers, chewed nails,

and I would forgive you
better if you left, and I lived.

First Blood

The dolls are bleeding,
all of them leaking,
red and black
from their forever open mouths,
what can we fill them with?
I don't like the way
they look at me
like they expect something more.
Since you've been gone,

they've started touching themselves,
running their plastic fingers
up their own shiny thighs,
I don't know how to stop them,
so I wait for you to come home,
whilst they slide their tongues
around their lips and look
at each other, eyes growing big.
Last night I filled an egg cup

with baking soda and vinegar,
and tried to clean their faces,
you were still gone,
they wouldn't let me near,
until I promised
to pour the vinegar away
and bleed with them, so I did,
legs touching, my bled fingerprints
forming like wax seals upon our skin.

Teenage Mother

they talk to me,
the day you were born,
as though another me stepped out
and never returned, my very own
double image, retreating, and for years I
only know knees of the dirty kind

hands which would struggle to pick up
a small stone, a halo fastened at the neck,
there is a world in which I never had you,
the handle to my parent's bedroom door
was missing, leaving behind a small
square eye hole, just above bed height.
I carried love around with me like milk
in a shallow bowl, watching it lapping the sides,
each drop bleaching my skin, there were days I broke

our home with only a few words,
I am not your mother.   Mother
has gotten itself stuck in my throat,
grown like a tumour or a foetus
but faster, from poppy seed to broad bean
until it's swollen so hard I can't

say anything more. In your bunk bed,
behind your back, I lie, holding on
to your plaited hair like a rope.

Portrait of My Mother as a Patient

Some days   I agree to live   with you
with your processed breath   and cigarettes
other days minutes pass only   with the renewed
heat   of your hand on my face   split
into quarters   I look like you   a quarter
I love you   a quarter   I hate you   the rest
is up to teachers   or vicars   or whoever
isn't still in bed   to teach me   *What is all this*
woman stuff for?   You keep your tomorrows
in small glass vials   with stretched   rubber lids
taut for piercing   collect needles   I sterilise
for you   *watch the way it blends*   you say
slowly   as though the powder   and the water
are a witch's spell   and you   finally
have some power   to pass on   but I
have always been there at the chemists   trying
not to breathe   the stale salty air they all breathe
out   watching the way the pharmacist   looks
at your small   grey face inside   your hood
the thin way   you smile at him   how he places
his God boxes   in a white paper bag   with one
motion of his hand   like Jesus   acknowledging
a crowd   then folds over the top   and slides
it over the counter toward you keeping his hands
far away.

Postnatal I

You came in the night   put your hands around her cheeks
and yanked her   from my nipple   or   if You didn't   You stole
all the food   fed Yourself   on the bread I baked   that afternoon
grew bigger   or   if not   You hid   in corners   stealing glances
of moments You called mistakes   warned everything would ruin
made me shiver   or   if that wasn't You   You were somewhere
all the time   getting closer   I could hear You whisper   feel my hair
parting for Your breath   and when You came to face us   I wouldn't say
You were   shadow   more the sharp winter light   stabbing
through the windscreen   on an early morning drive   sending me
swerving   burning   my eyes

Speak of The Devil

The counsellor said I couldn't talk to her
anymore about You. She said it wasn't her job
to tell me how to do things, but I was using
the commodity of her all wrong,

she was, from now on, doctoring
the availability of the vocabulary
within our shared language,
and completely removing You.

I spoke to her instead about the beach
we visited when I was younger, me in bare feet
and the bridge with pitted metal steps and no signs
anywhere, warning of the fluctuating tides

which engulfed the path in minutes,
and how sea water, thick, around the waist
feels like the boniest hands squeezing. I spoke
about the rosette ribbon tails

of the dove grey horse
we owned when I was sixteen, and how
he threw me over a fence so high, dad thought
there was no way I'd survive.

Miss Polly had a Dolly

Yesterday I ate one of the dolls,
she was rubbery and hard to chew

her small fists were bitter like cobnuts
and her eye lashes tickled my throat.

I had to be brave when I swallowed her hair.
It wasn't that there was nothing else to eat

it was that she wouldn't stop talking,
about how long it's been since you last

sat here on my bed, she wouldn't stop
turning my hands over and over in hers,

like playing cards, palms up, palms down,
face up, face down, she wouldn't stop

knowing what I know. I have your hands Mother
and I notice this most when I'm getting ready to eat.

Broken Waters

Most people drown
     without making
a noise or splashing. See me

here Baby, watch
     me lying
out plank, below the surface,

all that stillness, all that
     peace, see
how long I can breathe

down here alone. You must
     trust me,
I am your mother after all,

don't think about the firefighter
     who lies
to the woman on the phone inside

the burning building, says he's on his
     way up
to save her, then hands her brother

back the phone, *tell her you*
     love her,
knowing all his tears

won't be enough to quiet the
     flames, I am
your mother after all, I am made

to do this. When the mother harp seal
        leaves its cub,
nobody calls it a mistake,

I have been at this much longer than
        twelve days –
just let me float here a while, Baby

you will still remember my face.
        It will be
the same one you wear every time

life cuts in such a way – the serration
        drags the exact
formation of ripples upon its shape.

Postnatal II

You took away all the doors   so You could see
everything   without moving Your head   so the rooms
began smelling   the same   and all of You   the light bled
into new spaces   as though a sealed lid   had been broken
or a skull cracked open   it was no longer clear   if You
were in one place   or another   it didn't just mean   I had nowhere
to hide   it meant I could neither   keep You out   nor trap You
inside   and sometimes   I wonder   how it would have looked
if I'd tried   wrestling a ghost   and You   won't be called a ghost
and that's fine   just know that silently   I'm naming
new things   all the time

Thinking of My Mother as a Mother

of three little girls, and in that world
the third didn't die, and my mother
never came to know the exact necessary length

of a cord that's safe. In that world we are not
hungry, there is no collateral to our beauty, and my piano
lessons are not a curse, leading me to her funeral song.

My sister and I are not an interrupted
trilogy, a robbed, triple yolk, slipping
from the fractured shell we grew inside, and she,

she didn't have her lips painted red
for the photograph, the only one we have, the one
which, in this world lives, on top of my mother's

TV, the one I would stare at whole evenings
as a child. *A dead baby. A dead baby*, was all
I could think, *why, do we have a dead baby*

on top of the telly? until I had my own,
warm and soft, and realised
those sealed eyes, that china thin skin

was a living baby, turned porcelain,
my mother's own
perfectly painted doll, the only girl

she ever knew who didn't grow
to disappoint.

While I Was Feeding You

the sexless years were all   breasts
they were all
flopping cracked nipples   in front of parting
lips   all oral   all reflex

they were all   between-meal
jumpers bundled half-mast   flashes
of skin   top-section-only   desperate
meetings of impropriety   eyes

for no other   all hunger and thirst
they were spent

the way I was   drop by drop
into another's mouth   mostly
horizontal   always in love

Victoria Richards

Victoria Richards is a journalist and writer. In 2017/18 she was shortlisted in the Bath Novel Award and the Lucy Cavendish College Fiction Prize, was highly commended for poetry in the Bridport Prize and came third in *The London Magazine* Short Story Competition. She was also longlisted in the National Poetry Competition.

To be fifteen

and after the third can of Super Strongbow cider
to throw up in the bathroom belonging to that girl
in the year above, the one with the bra straps and dirty jokes.
She breathes in smoke without coughing, says, "alright?"
to the most beautiful boy at school, the most beautiful boy
with hair black as cats' tails, slippery as nicotine,
his smile a lopsided carousel.

To have only just started your period and to have your not-breasts
christened "pancake" by the boys who stand like gatekeepers
in the kitchen belonging to that girl. Rows on rows of teeth.
To have written a letter to the beautiful boy
and to have asked him, unthinkably, to read it.
To hear him say, "I like you – a *bit*,"
like that, *bit* in italics.

To leave traces of last night's dinner
all over the pale-pink shower suite belonging to that girl,
the one her parents picked from *Because You're Unique*
even though it starts with a subordinating conjunction.
To see her point, then say "that's her"
until it becomes a hurricane.
Her smile will tell its own story and she will call it truth.

Of sagging into the beautiful boy like he's the wind
and you a used tissue wearing someone else's mascara.
Of laughing chaotically at something he said
that was only half-funny, of touching his knee
and letting him touch yours, because knees are prayers
and fingers communion wafers. Of going with him
to the garden belonging to that girl. Of being ordained.

Of someone calling your parents and for your dad to come,
for him to climb the stairs belonging to that girl in silence,
force the lock while you lie foal-limbed –
to carry you out to the car like a trampled chrysanthemum.
Take you home, pull off your tights.
Wipe shame, hot and sticky, from your hair,
put a bin next to the bed for morning.

To be fifteen and to have to call the house belonging to that girl.
To say sorry through sheet glass over a tongue of sand,
to rip yourself raw. To go back to school on Monday,
toes curled and desperate inside ruby slippers two sizes too small.
Childhood taps you on the shoulder – *you're a woman, now!*
To pray for an outbreak of collective amnesia.
Of mass, unexplained cardiac arrest.

To the teenage girl sobbing at the bus stop

I don't give you my coat
though your shirt is translucent with rain,

glance sideways at the ballpoint tattoos
on the backs of your hands,

don't ask why you've scribbled out 'love'
and written 'sucks' instead.

I'm sorry if your friends left you to cry alone,
or someone tore your heart, made it ragged at the edges,

if the person who broke you didn't see the symmetry of your face –
your black-blunt fringe, teeth white and strong as horses.

I'm sorry if your mum couldn't take care of you, or was never
taught how, or if your dad loved whisky more.

I turn my back to get away from the sky's slow dripping –
Canary Wharf a lighthouse in the distance.

Rue d'Antibes

The silhouettes the Chinese artist created
were so lifelike they drew crowds.

He seemed to take something from everyone
who posed for him, fingers slicing, whirring.

Go on, my dad said, pushing me in front of his scissors.
He looked at me roughly and began to cut –

my outline stamped forever on black card.
Each year I came away a little less.

By fifteen, I'd lost both ears and the childish curve
of my chin. By sixteen, my lips. By seventeen, joy.

By eighteen, all that was left was scraps of black paper,
offcuts on the studio floor.

The whistle is missing from my life jacket

When he is born he is piscine slippery, grey and unearthly.
Black-button eyes frozen by shock-sudden roaring,
like suckerfish caught in a dull, red slipstream.

He ducks and slaps, blows bubbles,
panic-pulls blue cord that binds and breaks us and
I can't believe he's here.
Is he okay? Is he breathing?

I rest my head against the rim and wait for someone to shout
– man overboard –

Your gull cry pierces the night

We struggle in each other's arms as you twist and writhe,
reel backwards, lead me in a stilted dance across the ocean floor.

We bump against the box marked 'your first year', that changing mat
with the blue stripes, a yellow blanket, knitted by an aunt –

the shipwreck of your cot. I let the current drag me under
as bubble-wrap tentacles wave mournfully from the ceiling.

You are angry with me. You point at the door, *da da da,*
as my milk chokes in your throat. What more do I have to give?

They ripped my heart from my chest when you were born,
grafted it to your back with paste and a palette knife

while they stitched me back together. It bleeds openly,
that's why you sleep on your front, though you're not supposed to.

In the mornings your sheets are sodden red,
my blonde, bloodied, darling boy.

You are hungry. My tears won't fill you up –
they only fall in small, dark spaces when I read something sad

on my phone about young black kids being killed in America.
Take my mind, though you might not enjoy it much;

I left it behind at an 18-course tasting menu at The Dorchester.
There was foam and something called a velouté we paid £180 for

so pretended to love it, called it *rich and complex,*
narrowed our eyes and nodded. It left a strange, sour taste

in my mouth, emptied me inside-out. My body is hollow
but it's all I've got, and I don't know what else to feed you.

Lonely Planet gave this 4.6 stars out of 5

When you are sick, your hot breath smokes my cheek
like a furnace. Cygnet cry an unnatural swelling.
Crimson waves break over the edge of the bathtub,
tiny paper birds drown in the puddles.

I smooth your cotton hair, wear you in a ring sling –
one named 'festive skies'. My spine crumbles and collapses
like the Roman ruins we saw in Bulgaria, teeming with cats.
My hips move side-to-side in an endless mother sway.
"*Mama,*" you croak. "*Mama.*"

Unthinkably, I leave you

It is cold when my alarm goes off and I dress in the half-light
fingers fumbling laces, guts knotted like rope.
I haven't slept, not really.

Checked the time every hour, half-hoping and half-dreading
to hear that cough. I keep the door to your room open, space between us
stretching like a rubber band. It is dark, where you are.

In the pale pink of the baby monitor I see the elephant lampshade,
the wooden owl, hanging from the ceiling. Then I leave you
for the taxi waiting outside, the driver calling home to Pakistan.

I leave you for deadlines and for breaking news, to write
about the weather and other people's children, fighting for life
on the opposite side of the world.

I leave you for rotas, for responsibility. Sit at my desk for an hour
until my phone rings, my mother's panicky voice. Then – running
through the slow, revolving doors, out of New Broadcasting House,

down Portland Place, away from All Souls Church.
Past the black and navy suits marching from the underground,
vaulting the jagged escalator steps in threes to take the next train east.

The road home glitters with black ice, the crack and crunch
of snail shells beneath my feet. Blue lights bounce on the dark street:
to Gary and Phil in green uniforms, forging animals from puffed-up
    latex gloves,

to the hospital parking bay, to pushing our way into theatre
through swing doors. I kiss the bruises, mauve on white from the IVs
and think of the snails that were hurt as I ran.

They will find me in the street in my dressing gown

The next time I leave some of myself behind
in his cot or her hospital bed
they will find me in the street in my dressing gown.

Paving slabs splintered at my feet. Spoiled water the colour of rust –
the name I used to call myself written in chalk and washed away.
My heart burned to ash by the dreamers in the forest
naked beneath their terry-cloth crowns.

L'appel du vide

When I became a mother I lost myself (*active*), I got lost (*passive*)
my mind broke and I went mad, I was mental, you know?
I couldn't cope with the horror of loving this tiny thing so completely

it was like being INSIDE the news – like a hostage situation,
where I'm the gunman and the bullet at the same time,
where my life is narrated by David Attenborough, talking talking talking

as I am swallowed whole like a snake swallows a deer – inch by inch –
until the deer is no longer a deer, but a giant bulge in the snake's stomach,
and *Jesus Christ*, is it alive in there? Could it still be alive in there?

And on becoming a mother, after seven series of Gilmore Girls
while *baby* slept 23 hours of every day,
while *daughter* went to school and came home crying

because she had to make all new friends and couldn't hug me
because my hands were full of baby, my breasts so full of milk,
and it hurt for her to grip me tight with her pink-and-green bracelet arms.

After, they both got sick, heartbeats angry white-on-black:
170 – *no, you can't go home* –
200 – *we need to move you into resus* –

after that, a long time after that, while walking in the forest I realised
I hadn't thought about the autumn leaves. Hadn't noticed the gold
and red and soft brown crunch, or the swans

or that heron sitting on the post in his grey overcoat
or the dogs running sideways with the wind in their ears
or the bluebells in the woods that people travel for miles to see.

I hadn't spoken for days and I'd hardly eaten
and my mouth was a stone
and I lost myself somewhere between the bus stop and the A406

on that motorway bridge where traffic zooms by so fast it blurs –
and what's the word for the feeling when you stand too close to the edge
and get the uncontrollable urge to throw yourself off?

Milk Thistle

"Nikka from the Barrel is gorgeous," the barman says,
but he puts his hand on my knee and I taste smoke and confusion.

His fingers are hieroglyphs, each one a mollusc
suffocated by the rock it chose –

the rock it loved for a thousand years, covered in barnacles.
They are like those angler fish I read about, the ones with jagged teeth.

If I tilt my head in a certain way the feet of a couple on a first date
don't quite meet at the bar. He wears a black check bowtie;

she, a red-and-white ghost dress burned into her skin by the sun.
They steal glances as they steal sips of Champagne

while the women next to them talk without speaking, conversation like
mirrors. The barman brings them a drink but doesn't touch their knees

and I want – *What? What do you want?* –
to sit in the quiet dark, in a ghost dress of my own.

Ingrid Bergman

Ingrid Bergman is so beautiful that when I watch her in Casablanca
I want to peel her skin off and wear it as a coat.

Pluck out her eyes, like Goneril ordered Cornwall to do to Gloucester –
Leave him to my displeasure. I dream heavy, sexy dreams

of rolling one of Ingrid's eyes against my tongue like the gobstopper
I kept for weeks in a plastic pot of precious things:

stones pulled from a stream in South Africa, one sparkly button,
two baby teeth, a crumpled crisp packet dropped by the boy I loved.

Ingrid Bergman's glorious, gobstopper-eye makes my tongue ache
the way it aches when you eat pineapple, because of bromelain.

It lures you in with its sticky sweetness and eats you alive.
But Ingrid's eye doesn't last long. I just can't help those furtive licks.

It grows small and wrinkled, stops shining, and then the tears dry up.
Lost on a bed of sequins, prised from a cheap polyester coat.

My precious, precious things: a ring, a postcard, nail scissors, an old shell.
A letter from my father.

And a float shaped like the Starship Enterprise

Vancouver Pride, 2017

I watch them: incandescent in love, in glitter, neon tutus
around their waists like froth circling the rim of a coffee cup.

Vast expanse of desert skin, slick shimmering gold,
hair like scrub grass blurring the edges of a black ink heart.

I want to ask how it feels to love so openly, and if it hurts –
but a woman brushes past and steals the words from my tongue.

She wears a coat of painful nonchalance though she's naked
from the waist up, rough black tape across her nipples,

the swollen flesh beneath made sticky with hiding.
Her body flows away like water trying to escape, or maybe

her body is a dam? A man stands on tiptoe to kiss another man
taller, stronger, more handsome than he is.

And he knows it, that first man, wears the exquisite anticipation
of being left behind like lipstick.

Not yet, his thighs whisper, circling the tall man's waist. *Not yet.*
A stranger calls them "cute" and takes their picture

to stick in an album 5,000 miles away, to show he was here
on this day of noise and plastic water-bottle penises

with a spout in the end and rainbow sunglasses and PRETTY BOY
stamped across narrow chests and a girl in a pink t-shirt

with a unicorn on the front that neighs and whinnies and snorts
"I'm not gay – I'm *super* gay."

And I wonder if, years from now, the man who took that picture
will pull out the memory and turn to whoever is close enough

or cares enough to listen and say, *I was there.*
And point at a small man, reaching up to kiss a tall man.

This sad story will make you cry

A bridesmaid has a heart attack at her sister's £70,000 wedding
on the exact same fucking day a poet visits a nursing home.

A sea, the poet says. A sea of outstretched hands.
If that doesn't make you cry, nothing will.

In Australia, a woman with dementia disappears,
one neat pile of bones left next to the water.

And I wonder if she was trying to make a friend in that black lagoon,
or if she fell in love while gazing at her own reflection.

A team of scientists sends a Tunnock's teacake into space.
We're delighted, they say, over the moon! *I cry, I cry, I cry.*

I *don't* cry when the paramedics lie about the sirens, and they know I know.
Nothing to worry about, they say. Gets us there a bit faster, that's all.

I watch them: holding breaths, turning on the flashing lights,
swapping glances like lovers swap saliva as they shift into fourth gear.

I don't cry, sitting next to a hospital gurney while my love lies helpless,
chest moving up and down like an accordion played fast and wild.

I don't cry, pacing alone in an off-white cubicle for seven hours, listening
to the quiet unravelling of a fourteen-year-old girl with wrists like ribbons.

I once asked an eye doctor if red-hot lasers could make me see more clearly.
Want to know what he said?

Your tear ducts are so low, shaking his head.
You'll never have 20/20 vision.

This is my last will and testament

When the time comes for me to die, put me in a lobster suit
like the guy at the end of the London Marathon, for there is always that guy.
Doughy flesh hidden by foam and latex, smile wide and cheering.

He pays extra for comfort ventilation panels, a built-in cooling fan,
googly eyes (on springs). Claw mittens. A separate headpiece.
If I could spend just one day inside that suit, I would die happy.

Listen: pour boiling water over me, press the lid of the pan down tight,
steam-clean my secrets. Put your fingers in your ears to drown
out my high-pitched whistling. Watch my white-blue flesh turn pink.

Notes and Acknowledgements

Lewis Buxton:
The italics in 'Advice from the Quarterback' are extracts from Clint Trickett's interview in *The New York Times* in November 2015 and reported speech from his appearance in the documentary series *Last Chance U*. Sevenlings are a form based on the work of Anna Akhmatova, they consist of 7 lines and 3 stanzas. The first two stanzas should each contain lists of 3 things, and the final stanza should act as narrative summary, punchline or an unusual juxtaposition. Sevenlings are usually simply titled 'Sevenling'. In 'Frightened Rabbit' there is a quotation from Goethe, *'every colour does some violence to the eye'*, which also appears in Maggie Nelson's *Bluets*. 'Red Shirt' is written in response to Robert Pinsky's poem 'Shirt' from *The Figured Wheel: New and Collected Poems 1966-1996* (Farrar Straus and Giroux, 1996). In 'Nom-de-guerre' the quotation from Tiffany Atkinson comes from *Kink and Particle* (Seren, 2006).

Victoria Richards:
'Unthinkably, I leave you' was highly commended in the Bridport Prize 2017, and published in the prize anthology. 'The whistle is missing from my life jacket' was first published in the online literary magazine *Cease, Cows* in May, 2018. 'Your gull cry pierces the night' was first published as 'Weaning' in *Please Hear What I'm Not Saying,* an anthology for Mind. 'L'appel du vide' was recorded and broadcast in February 2018 as part of the 100 Voices for 100 Years project, celebrating women's suffrage. (http://www.100voicesfor100years.com/voice-of-the-day/2018/2/6/introduction-or-what-ill-say-when-i-read-the-poem).